A 7-DAY MOTIVATIONAL

journal

Designed To Get You Through Each Day of The Week

How to use this journal

Rather than simply going from beginning to end, move freely through the journal, as you feel led. I've included Sections, with the "prompts" that helped me through my journey.

What is Your Why Today?

Specific Prompts for:

Mondays

Tuesdays

Wednesdays

Thursdays

Fridays

Saturdays

Sundays

As you are inspired each day, simply write in the section that applies to your mood.

This is My Why

Boy oh boy! We thought the pandemic was a roller coaster ride. However, the year 2022 bought many trials and tribulations in my life. It gave me the unruly feeling that I would never see the light at the end of the tunnel. Many grave mistakes led to a stray path. As life is all about experiencing the yin and the yang, my yang moments forced me to learn that I was sabotaging my own light and the gifts that God blessed me with.

Have you ever felt caged mentally, physically, financially, spiritually, or all of the above throughout your life journey? Speaking from personal experiences, my darkest days led me to hit rock bottom. Day after day, it felt like the walls were closing in on me. Every day felt so routine. Books such as "Daily Bread" and "Faith to Faith" helped save my life. Being able to pick up those motivational books every day meant everything to me. It even gave me the strength to keep going.

Now I am writing my own journal. Except, this time I am free. You too can get another chance to create opportunities for yourself. I pray this 7- day journal will give you the motivation to turn your pain into passion, fears into faith, trials into triumphs, dreams into success, and depression into happiness and love.

ONCE YOU KNOW YOUR WHY, YOU CAN SURVIVE ANYTHING!

How would you define your "why" in life? What is your why?

Date:

What legacy do you want to leave behind?

Date:

What things are you doing or working toward now that are helping to shape the legacy you want to leave?

____

____

____

____

____

____

____

____

____

____

____

____

____

____

____

____

MAYBE THIS DAY IS NOT ONE OF YOUR FAVORITES, BUT NEVER FORGET THAT EVERY DAY YOU WAKE UP IS AN AMAZING GIFT AND IT'S UP TO YOU TO MAKE IT OUT.

What are you grateful for today and why?

Date:

THIS IS YOUR MONDAY MORNING REMINDER THAT YOU CAN HANDLE WHATEVER THIS WEEK THROWS AT YOU.

What are some challenges you hope to overcome today?

Date:

MONDAYS ARE THE START OF THE WEEK WHICH OFFER NEW BEGINNINGS 52 TIMES A YEAR!

What are some things you will do this week that you have never done before?

Date:

____

____

____

____

____

____

____

____

____

____

____

____

____

____

____

Every morning you have two choices: continue to sleep with your dreams or wake up and chase them.

What skills would you like to improve today? How will improving these skills help you better succeed?

Date:

____

____

____

____

____

____

____

____

____

____

____

____

____

____

____

____

TUESDAY IS THE AFFIRMATION THAT YOUR GOALS ARE BEING MOVED ANOTHER STEP FORWARD.

What goals do you need to accomplish today? How are you going to accomplish your goals?

Date:

____
____
____
____
____
____
____
____
____
____
____
____
____
____
____
____

HAPPY TUESDAY! KEEP YOUR CIRCLE POSITIVE. SPEAK GOOD WORDS. THINK GOOD THOUGHTS. DO GOOD DEEDS.

What good have you done today? What good have you seen someone else do today?

Date:

HAVE A BEAUTIFUL TUESDAY! YOUR MANTRA IS: 'ALL I HAVE IS ALL I NEED AND ALL I NEED IS ALL I HAVE IN THIS MOMENT.'

What are some of your talents (hidden or otherwise) that makes you, you?

Date:

____

____

____

____

____

____

____

____

____

____

____

____

____

____

____

____

____

HAPPY TUESDAY! DECIDE WHAT YOU WANT. BELIEVE YOU CAN HAVE IT. BELIEVE YOU DESERVE IT AND BELIEVE IT'S POSSIBLE FOR YOU.

Why is believing in yourself so important and how do you do it?

Date:

What components of self-belief do you struggle with? (self-worth, self-confidence, self-trust, etc.)

Date:

THERE ARE TIMES WE NEED TO SET ASIDE OUR FEELINGS AND JUST GO FOR IT. MAKE THIS WEDNESDAY ONE OF THOSE TIMES.

**What do you have to
make time for today?**

Date:

HAPPY WEDNESDAY! YOU ARE WHO YOU ARE; BE HAPPY WITH WHAT YOU ARE CALLED TO DO. DO NOT PRETEND TO BE LIKE SOMEONE ELSE FOR YOUR GIFTS ARE UNIQUE TO HELP LEAD YOU TO THE SUCCESS AS ONLY YOU CAN DEFINE. HAVE A GOOD DAY.

What are your values, and are you being true to them today?

Date:

WEDNESDAY WILL EITHER MAKE YOU OR BREAK YOU. YOU ARE EITHER ON THE UPWARD TREND OR THE DOWNWARD SLIDE TO THE END OF THE WORK WEEK. GIVE IT ALL YOU'VE GOT THIS WEDNESDAY!

In what ways have you promoted physical, mental and spiritual wellbeing today?

WHAT YOU GO THROUGH
EACH DAY DOESN'T
DEFINE YOUR WORTH.
NEVER LET A BAD DAY BE THE
EXCUSE TO
STOP TRYING. BETTER
DAYS ARE COMING AND
ALWAYS REMEMBER THAT
YOU ARE WORTHY.

What motivates you to get out of bed in the morning?

Date:

REASONS TO BE HAPPY ON THURSDAY

YOU ONLY HAVE THURSDAY <u>ONCE</u>

YOU MAKE IT THROUGH <u>MONDAY</u>, TUESDAY, AND WEDNESDAY

TOMORROW IS <u>FRIDAY</u>

How do you make each day count?

Date:

IT'S THURSDAY! BE THANKFUL FOR WHAT YOU ARE NOW AND KEEP FIGHTING FOR WHAT YOU WANT TO BE TOMORROW.

How do you plan to
better yourself today?

Date:

MAKE IT YOUR GOAL TO MAKE SOMEONE SMILE ON THIS THURSDAY BY SHOWING A SMALL ACT OF KINDESS, YOU COULD CHANGE A PERSON'S LIFE IN A WAY YOU MAY NOT EVEN REALIZE.

In what ways do you make people smile throughout your day?

Date:

THURSDAY IS ONE DAY CLOSER TO EXPECTATION THAT EVERYTHING YOU HAVE DONE THROUGH THE WEEK CULMINATES IN PROGRESS.

What are some good things that happened so far this week?

Date:

WHEN YOU START TO DO THE THINGS THAT YOU TRULY LOVE, IT DOESN'T MATTER WHAT DAY OF THE WEEK IT IS. WHETHER IT IS MONDAY OR FRIDAY; YOU SHOULD BE EXCITED TO WAKE UP EACH MORNING TO WORK ON YOUR PASSIONS.

How do you deal with your regrets and successes on a day to day basis?

Date:

____

____

____

____

____

____

____

____

____

____

____

____

____

____

____

____

I CHALLENGE YOU TO LET EVERY DAY BE A FRIDAY. PERMIT YOURSELF TO BE HAPPY EVERY DAY.

What would entering a healthier relationship with yourself look like?

Date:

HIT THE RESET BUTTON. WHAT HAPPENED YESTERDAY, FORGET ABOUT IT. GET A NEW PERSPECTIVE. TODAY IS A NEW DAY. START FRESH, BEGIN NOW.

How do you support your mental health? How do you cope with it?

Date:

WHEN LIFE PUTS YOU IN A TOUGH SITUATION DON'T SAY 'WHY ME' JUST SAY 'TRY ME'. HAVE A PRODUCTIVE FRIDAY.

Who do you lean on during your time of need?

Date:

HAVE A GREAT SATURDAY! EXPERIENCE LIFE IN ALL POSSIBLE WAYS: GOOD-BAD, BITTER-SWEET, DARK-LIGHT, SUMMER-WINTER. DON'T BE AFRAID OF EXPERIENCE, BECAUSE THE MORE EXPERIENCE YOU HAVE, THE MORE MATURE YOU BECOME.

What do you hope to experience today?   **Date:**

FORGET ALL THE BAD MEMORIES OF A WEEK THAT'S ALREADY GONE. PREPARE YOURSELF FOR YET ANOTHER BEAUTIFUL WEEK THAT STARTS WITH A DELIGHTFUL SATURDAY EXPERIENCE. HAPPY SATURDAY!

What are you looking forward to doing this weekend?

Date:

THE WORD "SATURDAY" HAS THE WORD "SAT" IN IT. MAKE SURE YOU TAKE THE TIME THIS DAY TO SIT AND RELAX.

Write down some positive interactions you've had this week

Date:

OH! IT'S SATURDAY AGAIN. SHARE THE LOVE THAT WAS MISSING DURING THE WEEK, IN A WORTHY MOMENT OF PEACE AND BLISS.

What are you still learning about yourself?

Date:

START THIS SUNDAY WITH A CLEAN HEART. NO DOUBTS. NO TEARS. NO FEARS. NO WORRIES. THANK GOD FOR HIS PRICELESS GIFTS AND MIRACLES.

Free write, express yourself!   Date:

Free write, express yourself!   Date:

Free write, express yourself!

Date:

Free write, express yourself!   Date:

Free write, express yourself!   Date: